Tooley Transformation Training
2742 San Ramon Drive
Rancho Palos Verdes, CA 90275
310-832-0830
Email: life@duncantooley.com

DISCLOSURE:
The author's expression of his convictions and practices are unrelated to any board game. Free use of the material is encouraged with written permission required for quotation beyond three paragraphs. The reader is responsible for evaluation and use of the author's viewpoint, lived experiences, and applied mentor wisdom in their journey as Player in the Real Game of Life.

ACKNOWLEDGEMENTS:
Acknowledgement and appreciation goes to mentors Brother Felician Fourrier, S.C., Brother Pierre St. Pierre, S.C., Mike Dooley, James Wanless, Dr. Wayne Dyer, Dr. Shelley Stockwell-Nicholas, Louise Hay, Abraham-Hicks, Marianne Williamson, Soaring Eagle, and for encouragement from Dr. Leyla Ali, Dr. Aviva Boxer, Dr. Virginia Upton, Al Delaney, and my family and friends.

ISBN: 978-0-9983323-6-9

Copyright © 2024 Duncan Tooley
All rights reserved

LIFE's
PLAYBOOK

The Real GAME-of-LIFE INSTRUCTIONS

How to Attract FUN, MONEY, & MIRACLES

Duncan Tooley

Dedication

Dear Reader,

I'm having so much fun playing at life and creating miracles that I want to share with you how I do it. I wrote these instructions as the guide I follow to play my *Game of Life.* You can create your own magic results by following the missing *Life Instructions* I eventually found.

I know you can achieve this because my mentors predicted it for me, I experience it every day, and I have seen it work in the lives of others.

I dedicate this guide to players of all ages in Life's Game who wish to experience the fun, adventure, and joy that we all deserve as our birthright on planet Earth. It's time to have the fun we intended when we came.

My love and blessings. Let's play!

Duncan

Table of Contents

1. Life's A Game 1
2. Game-of-Life Instructions 4
3. Game-of-Life Playing Field 7
4. Game-of-Life Equipment 12
5. Game-of-Football Laws 18
6. Game-of-Life Laws 21
7. Game-of-Life Law of Attraction 22
8. Game-of-Life Law of Bipolarity 33
9. Game-of-Life Law of Diversity 37
10. Game-of-Life Law of Expansion 42
11. Game-of-Life Creator 45
12. Game-of-Life Players 48
13. Life Emotion Frequency Scale 65
14. Game-of-Life Rule #1 72
15. Game-of-Life Rule #2 75
16. Game-of-Life Rule #3 77
17. Game-of-Life GamePlay 78
18. Game-of-Life Scoring 88
19. Game-of-Life Referee 90
20. Game-of-Life Skills 93
21. Game-of-Life Coach 100
22. Game-of-Life Transformation 103
23. Game-of-Life Legacy 106
24. Game-of-Life HACK 108
25. Postscript 111
About the Author 112
Extra Game Emotion Frequency Scale 114

1. Life's A Game

In the Bronx apartment project where I grew up, there were no grassy fields to play ball. We boys invented a competitive game called *Skully,* like billiards with the play table and "pockets" chalked on the playground asphalt.

After carefully melting crayons into a bottle cap, I spent many fun hours with my friends building the skill to flick my bottlecap with thumb and forefinger into the next pocket or at

1

1. Life's A Game

least knock another player's piece out of the way.

I've played lots of fun games over my eighty-five years. They were so much fun because it's how *life* is meant to be. Life itself is a huge sacred multi-player game designed for great fun, pleasure, and joy. We are made to have fun in the GAME of Life.

To have fun means to discover, explore, and learn by experience. Pleasure in the Game comes from the freedom to choose, pursue, and create things I like, to be and do and have whatever I desire.

Joy comes from the opportunity to experience freedom, creativity, beauty, and love, and to return another's love.

1. Life's A Game

No game is fun if players don't know the rules of the game and how to follow them. Learning how to play is essential for success and fun in all games, especially in the Game of Life.

Every human is a simultaneous player in Life's Game. This little book contains everything each player needs for maximum success, fun, and joy in Life's Game.

The laws and rules apply equally to every aspect of life from having fun, attracting material things, like money, jobs, cars, and people, like friends and lovers, and creating miracles of all types. All of these are ready, queued up and waiting for us to summon them.

2. Game-of-Life Instructions

Emotions filled my years, mostly fun and happiness, but also serious searching for the cause and meaning behind the experiences I didn't like. For eight decades, I thought it unfair that life came without an instruction manual.

Now that I understand life better, I'm having more fun and get beyond the bumps more easily and quickly. I see the wisdom in the structure of Life's game.

2. Game-of-Life Instructions

We get to sample whatever we desire to learn from each experience. We build personal stamina and clarity as we cut our own path through the jungle without the aid of a road, trail, or map but with a built-in guidance system.

The light to understand my life experiences in a way that led to writing these instructions came from my teachers and mentors, my inner guide, and inspired downloads.

I now know I jumped into this lifetime at this time and place to have fun learning and doing the things I like. I hoped to reap a heap of joy and satisfaction in each interaction in the *Game of Life*. Through twists and turns, I've learned what works to keep me young, healthy, and having fun.

I prepared this instruction manual initially for my grandchildren. My desire is that it will benefit them to understand their life experiences and to take the controls to design their future.

2. Game-of-Life Instructions

You are reading this Playbook of Instructions because early readers encouraged me to share my story of discovery learning how to play the *Game of Life.*

May it serve as a lens for you to view your life and unlock all the fun, adventure, and joy you deserve as your birthright on planet Earth.

Life is a GAME. Enjoy the fun!

3. GAME-OF-LIFE PLAYING FIELD

A game's playing field is the environs in which the game is played. The world's most popular game, football, (soccer in America, Canada, and Australia), requires a net-covered, white-pipe goal at each end of a grassy field.

The Game of Life is played by every soul on planet Earth in every kind of physical setting. Its defining field is an invisible web of limitless flowing energy that permeates space and time by delivering life force to everything in existence.

3. Game-of-Life Playing Field

Energy powers the universe. Nuclear fusion in the sun releases energy as sunlight that plants convert to chemical energy in food. Our body converts food to electrical energy running the brain, heart, and gut, and into mechanical and thermal energy in the body's muscles.

In Life's Game, we play directly with *energy* through our thoughts, imagination, and actions.

I call life's vibrating energy field *THE-FLOW*. It is as pervasive as the electromagnetic energy waves that permeate all space. It is just as real as your cell phone connection but infinitely more powerful. *THE-FLOW* is the deliberately organized playing field of conscious energy, the field of abundance, life force, and well-being that powers Life's Game.

3. Game-of-Life Playing Field

THE-FLOW is called *Prana* in yoga and Hindu, *chi* by the Chinese, *mana* by the Polynesians, *Qi* by the Japanese, the *Unified Field of Consciousness* by quantum physicists, and *the Force* in the Star Wars sagas.

THE-FLOW is creative energy. It powered the Big Bang creation of the time-space universe. It is the dark energy accelerating the galaxies away from each other. It matches people, events, and circumstances by their vibration frequencies in perfect timing to deliver expected game results.

When I taught high school physics, I would use an ordinary iron nail to illustrate an energy field. The nail's atoms vibrate in a jumbled orientation like a fistful of toothpicks dropped on the floor.

When the nail is stroked in the same direction repeatedly with a pole magnet, the individual iron atoms rotate until they align. The previously jumbled

3. Game-of-Life Playing Field

atoms morph into another magnet as they orient themselves in the same direction.

The effect of their magnetic field is revealed by sprinkling iron filings onto a piece of paper with the new magnet-nail underneath.

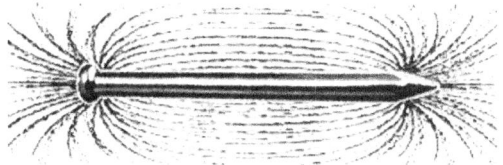

Our Game of Life playing field is a similar energy field but infinitely more powerful, extending throughout the universe and intersecting with our personal radiated energy field.

We will always be playing with the energy of our thoughts interacting with the consciousness energy of the Universe. Life's game is powered by matched frequency. The greater the frequency match of the energy vibrations, the more creative the results produced from this synergy.

3. Game-of-Life Playing Field

I am a vibrating being sending out energy that is creating my future experiences. I am causing either my wanted or my unwanted future by my thoughts right now depending on their frequency.

Miracles are the normal results of frequency-matched energy flow. They are considered *sacred* because they were once believed to be beyond possibility. They are possible for us because we can create extraordinary things with our thought energy as easily as we create ordinary things.

4. GAME-OF-LIFE EQUIPMENT

The game of football (soccer) uses an air-filled ball as its only equipment. I've learned that Life's Game equipment is the *ENERGY* radiating from our complex of Body, Mind, and Spirit that interacts with the *THE-FLOW,* field of consciousness energy.

Our *BODY* is an energy processor of trillions of specialized cells. Millions of sensory neurons send a constant flow of information about our internal and external environment to the brain, stimulating billions of neurons to send instructions to organs and muscles.

4. Game-of-Life Equipment

The flow of electrochemical signals between neurons generates electrical waves causing our whole body to emit a detectable energy aura.

My mentors told me I was already plugged into the universal attractive energy field of abundance and well-being that powers the Game of Life. They said I would attract my every desire when I aligned the frequency of the energy radiating from my heart and mind to my desires.

4. Game-of-Life Equipment

They told me *thought energy brings matched returns in the Game.* They said those who think about wealth get richer, those who appreciate their blessings get even more, and those who imagine their ideal relationship find their perfect partner.

They also said those who think they are poor get more poverty, those who talk of their illness get more sickness, and those who fear for their safety attract incidents they do not like. Those who focus on love, joy, and appreciation, attract happiness and fulfillment of their desires.

My teachers said these effects follow from the vibration energy everything in the universe emits and receives.

Although we are all in a constant shower of vibrations, only those with the same energy frequency as our

4. Game-of-Life Equipment

thoughts and emotions have any effect on us. We have invited their match.

When I aligned myself with this energy field, I discovered I became a magnet for things I wanted, just as my mentors told me would happen.

The ocean-overlook California home I dreamed about from Louisiana appeared unexpectedly on a trip with my wife, Dona, to San Pedro for a hypnosis class. It came fully remodeled *with the bow on top,* as Dona wished after our previous years-long remodel. The financing fell into place as if a genie worked behind the scenes. I've been able to enjoy the view of Santa Catalina Island for the past eighteen years.

4. Game-of-Life Equipment

Dona's lifetime of play on this planet ended after our forty-six years together. After I grieved and found my new connection to her post-Earth existence, I made a list of my desires to pursue art for the remainder of my time on Earth.

As you will learn further into these instructions, the energy of those deires attracted artist-author Eva to cross my path the following Valentine's Day. She brought identical books, heritage, interests, mentors, and certainty about how the Game of Life works based on her own life experiences.

As we flow toward our sixth year as *newlyweds* and play our Game of Life together, *THE-FLOW* surrounds

4. Game-of-Life Equipment

us, lights the way, and continues to surprise and delight us with the discovery of new energy matches and manifestations each day.

I see the beginnings of success blooming in my grandchildren who have taken to heart the words I put in a Christmas gift painting for each of them, *Seek joy first, and all good things will be added.*

I know it can be the same for you, dear reader, because the Game-of-Life laws and rules are the same for everyone, designed to bring miracles of joy and abundant satisfaction of all our desires.

🌀 🌀 🌀

5. GAME-OF-FOOTBALL LAWS

The environment of a game imposes constraints on how the game is played. These factors are called the *Laws* of the game because they affect every player equally and cannot be avoided.

Football is affected by four laws: Newton's three Laws of Motion and the Law of Universal Gravity:

1) Objects remain at rest or move in a straight line unless acted upon by an outside force.

2) Force equals mass multiplied by acceleration.

3) For every action (force), there is an equal and opposite reaction.

5. Game-of-Football Laws

4) Objects attract one another based on their masses and proximity (Law of Gravity).

The laws cause these effects in a game of football:

- The speed and distance of a kicked ball are proportional to the kicking mass (kicker's leg, foot, and shoe). The faster that mass hits the ball, the faster and the farther it will travel (*Newton's second and third laws*).

- Air friction will cause the kicked ball to slow, and it will be pulled down to the ground. *(Newton's first law and law of gravity).*

5. Game-of-Football Laws

No soccer player has any choice about the application of these laws. They are a universal aspect of football game play because they are built into the mechanics of the game on this planet. Whatever a player's skill, age, nationality, or team identity, these four laws always affect their every kick in the game.

If playing football (or watching it) is fun for you, you are playing the Game of Life well at those times because fun is the objective of Life's Game.

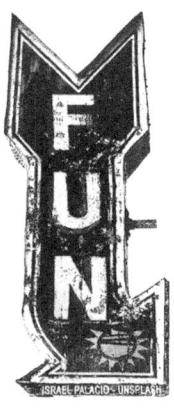

⚽ ⚽ ⚽

6. Game-of-Life Laws

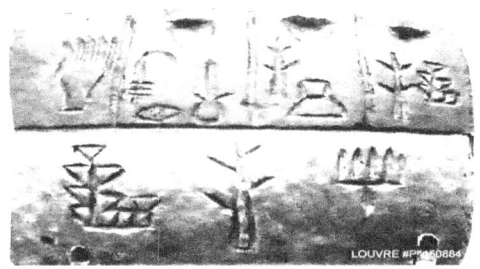

The Game of Life also has four structural laws that are embedded in the physics and metaphysics of Earth's play environment. Aspects of Life's laws can be seen, yet other parts are beyond what can be explained with science and physical mechanics.

Life's laws apply without exception to every player in Life's Game, even to those who are ignorant of them, deny them, or pretend they don't apply:

- The Law of Attraction
- The Law of Bipolarity
- The Law of Diversity
- The Law of Expansion

7. GAME-OF-LIFE LAW OF ATTRACTION

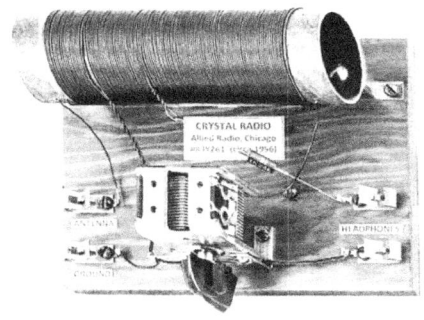

Students assembled a crystal radio as their first electronics experiment when I taught physics. It takes only three simple components to make a radio tuner that selectively pulls from among the many radio frequencies available only the station chosen by turning the dial to adjust the tuning frequency.

The simple crystal radio illustrates the first law of the Game of Life because we players in the Game are vibrational beings, and the Law of Attraction works much like a radio tuner.

7. Game-of-Life Law of Attraction

> **LAW of ATTRACTION:**
> Thoughts attract more same frequency energy.

From the many frequencies of energy around us, the Law tunes to deliver only the energy frequency of my thought at that moment. The Law does not know or care whether I am thinking about what I want or thinking about its absence that I do *not* want. It brings more of the same energy frequency as whatever I am thinking.

After a quarter minute of thought on a single topic, I begin to vibrate at the frequency of the thought. That radiated energy begins to attract similar thoughts. *THE-FLOW* brings more of the energy frequency I radiate.

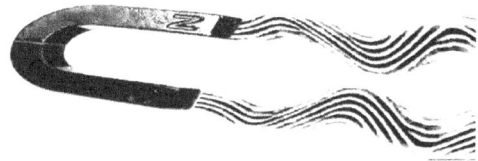

7. Game-of-Life Law of Attraction

A full minute of focused attention initiates the process for delivery of the manifestation of the physical reality that matches my vibration.

When I think, speak, or write about a subject, I am instructing the Law: *Go find and bring me more of similar energy.*

One of my mentors puts it simply: **Thoughts become things.**

Just as the momentum of a vehicle increases the longer it accelerates (Newton's Laws of Motion), my attractive momentum accelerates the longer I focus on a thought (Law of Attraction).

I like the buffer of time between initial thought and the beginnings of the physical manifestation because it permits me to change my thought in case my thought is about something I don't want.

7. Game-of-Life Law of Attraction

The Law of Attraction first got my attention in San Pedro, California when Dona and I had come to attend our second week-long class. Early Sunday morning, I searched for the bakery with delicious pastries I had found on the prior trip.

When I did not find the bakery, I began a pattern of searching the empty streets. I really wanted to find that bakery. Hungrier by the minute, I could almost taste the bear-claws as I envisioned biting into one in the bakery.

As I walked, I noticed a small blank white card on the sidewalk. I followed the impulse to pick it up and turn it over, revealing the bakery business card with its address. I easily found my bear-claws.

I had vaguely heard of the Law of Attraction, but that was my first realization of it working in my life. I now know, strange as it sounds, it was

7. Game-of-Life Law of Attraction

my powerful concentration on my desire to find the bakery that caused that card to be in my path.

I don't know how or when it got there. I have since concluded that figuring out how the Law of Attraction causes things to happen is beyond human minds. I just happily accept the results.

I've learned that when I have some discomfort or pain, if I focus on how much it hurts and how bad I feel, I get more of the same and feel worse. The sooner I change my focus to how good I am already feeling, the faster the pain or discomfort ends.

Thinking about or protesting things I don't want radiates their frequency and causes them to show up even more.

Instead of protesting things I dislike, I ignore them and become instead an advocate, promoter, and an energy radiator of what I *do* want.

7. Game-of-Life Law of Attraction

I tell my students and clients to think of the Law of Attraction as their personal creative energy magnet pulling toward them persons, events, things, emotions, actions matched to the frequency of their thoughts.

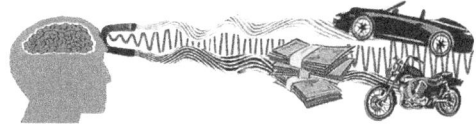

Their emanating thought energy affects not only their emotions and their body, but it also affects every other consciousness energy in the universe.

I had never heard *Your Mind Controls Your Body* until my first hypnotherapy training class. At the time, I had been on medical leave for many months with non-diabetic neuropathy (numb feet) that led to random falls. I had biweekly

7. Game-of-Life Law of Attraction

hospital IVIG infusions to prevent my immune system from further destroying the nerve sheaths in my feet. The nerve biopsy showed a few nerve chains where it should have been like a coaxial cable with thousands of wire-like neurons. I was told my existing nerve loss would be permanent.

After that hypnosis class, I began daily self-hypnosis giving my feet the instruction: *Nerve cells, grow back! Ignore the doctors who say you cannot. Immune system, leave the nerves alone!*

I felt better after five weeks. I quit the infusions and kept feeling better without falling. I had difficulty believing that my autosuggestion process had such a dramatic medical effect.

I wanted proof that it was not a coincidence and began searching for medical studies where hypnosis was the therapy tested. I found hundreds of studies with beneficial results on many different kinds of illnesses. That's when I changed my life's work from computer technology to hypnotherapy.

7. Game-of-Life Law of Attraction

Jane was among my first clients. She suffered pain from chronic non-diabetic neuropathy for ten years, took multiple narcotics daily, had spent thousands on ineffective treatments, and was becoming depressed. Her relief from using my simple mental process enabled her to stop taking six Norco (codeine) tablets a day. Her physician husband couldn't understand how or why it worked.

I have witnessed hundreds of similar results with many different illnesses. I now understand hypnotherapy is an application of the Law of Attraction. Whatever we desire strongly, believe is possible, and expect with emotion will always manifest. It is the Law!

Once I understood this, miracles have been easy. I will save for another time the story of my conversation with doctors as they performed my hernia surgery without anesthesia.

7. Game-of-Life Law of Attraction

My favorite is remote manipulation of the Louisville sorting system at UPS where shipments are sorted and routed.

Because I enjoy the affirmations from *Power Thoughts* by Louise Hay, I ordered a dozen books to bring to Louisiana as Christmas gifts for each of my grandchildren. My quickest delivery option had the books arrive the day after my flight.

I strongly desired to hand deliver them, so I imagined the shipment would get pushed off the conveyor sorting system at UPS into the *next-day* delivery route instead of its scheduled routing a day later. I envisioned watching my package move along the conveyor belts, saw it (in my mind's eye) pushed off the belt, and trusted it would get to me in time.

When I opened the front door to leave for the airport the next day, the package was on the front step. The Laws work like magic when a Game player works with them.

7. Game-of-Life Law of Attraction

Once, as I was reciting familiar instructions to a client under hypnosis, my words came out scrambled. The doctor from the adjacent office called 911. My hospital ER visit did not detect a stroke, the likely suspect, and the urgent matter was closed. However, a heart murmur was detected in the tests.

Weeks later, a cardiologist told me I had a malformed mitral heart valve that would not fully close. It needed a surgical repair or replacement with a pig heart valve.

I asked, *What if I do nothing?* His reply was *Your heart will expand to compensate for its drop in efficiency and will eventually expand enough to eliminate the possibility of a future valve replacement.*

7. Game-of-Life Law of Attraction

I didn't like that answer, so I chose to find a different cardiologist and to encourage my valve to straighten itself. My new cardiologist agreed to delay surgery and reevaluate my condition in twelve months.

I confidently encouraged my valve to improve, telling my family the next exam would show improvement even though the doctor said it was not possible.

He couldn't detect (or perhaps couldn't admit) improvement after the next year's exam. Now, after six years of annual exam comparisons, he has admitted improvement and reduced the diagnosis. I attribute the miracle of impossible improvement to learning to play the Game by envisioning desirable outcomes and leaving the results to the Law of Attraction.

This process works for every Life Game player. It will work for you, dear reader-player.

⚽ ⚽ ⚽

8. Game-of-Life Law of Bipolarity

Humans invented words to talk of absence in the same way we talk about *reality*. For example, we speak of light and darkness.

- *Light* is vibrating electromagnetic energy. Light is real, with measurable effects in plants and on skin and solar cells.

- *Darkness* is the abstract concept *absence of light*. Darkness cannot be measured and has no effects because it is not real or tangible. It's only an idea, an invented word for an absence.

8. Game-of-Life Law of Bipolarity

Similarly, we invented *night* for the absence of daylight; *poor* for the absence of money; *hunger* for the absence of nourishment; *naked* for the absence of clothes; *clean* for the absence of dirt; *homeless* for the absence of shelter; *empty* for the absence of anything filling; *dry* for the absence of moisture; *cold* for the absence of thermal energy (heat) . . . and the list continues to illustrate the bipolar nature of energy in the universe.

Both the absence of a substance and the real presence of the substance have vibrational energy, but the vibrational frequencies are different.

8. Game-of-Life Law of Bipolarity

> **LAW of BIPOLARITY:**
> Every topic has two closely related but distinct energies: The *reality* vibrating at one frequency and its (often abstract) *absence* vibrating at another frequency.

Example: The topic of money has two distinct vibrations: the thought of having plenty of money (the reality of having it available to spend now) generates a high-frequency pleasant emotion, but the thought of not having enough money (the absence of it), generates low-frequency emotions of anxiety or fear.

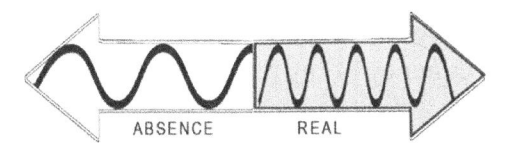

8. Game-of-Life Law of Bipolarity

My mind is my magic wand sending out energy waves (thoughts) to find matching energy. I always feel better, which means I am playing Life's Game better, when I think of what I want and avoid thinking of its absence or scarcity.

When I hold my magic wand at one end and think of what I want, my wishes come true, and miracles occur.

When I mistakenly wave my wand while holding the other end by thinking of what I don't want, I summon the absence of my desires. The Universal law of Attraction will then deliver more *absence* because it always delivers whatever matches the frequency of my thoughts.

👁 👁 👁

9. GAME-OF-LIFE LAW OF DIVERSITY

The Universe has a mandate of *"More, different, forever!"* Expansion causes change, variety, and evolution, producing all the diversity around us.

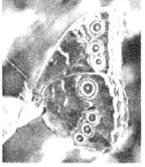

There are 17,500 species of butterflies; dozens of skin colors; thousands of shoe styles; millions of different faces; hundreds of sauces; billions of unique finger whorls; and ten thousand religions.

9. Game-of-Life Law of Diversity

> **LAW of DIVERSITY:**
> Variety, difference, diversity, and contrast are essential factors in Life's Game.

Humanity's differences in race, size, shape, behavior, disposition, opinions, speech, customs, and food preferences are all forms of diversity.

Life is a team sport. I need other people, even if they are different, like different things, or disagree with me. Diversity leads to contrast, a striking difference between two things when compared. It provides freedom to choose what I like and prevents the boredom of sameness.

I notice the diversity and contrast around me. Dozens of sauces and condiments line the shelves in a large grocery store. Many I would never buy. Some sound disgusting to me, but someone likes and buys them.

9. Game-of-Life Law of Diversity

I can ignore them; their presence doesn't affect me. Having more choices benefits everyone.

Although the words *good* and *bad* often arise when people talk about diversity, the Game of Life never uses these words.

I found the words *good* and *bad* make more sense when I interpret them this way:

- *Good* means I prefer or desire it; I like it; I want it; I am pleased with it; it makes me happy.
- *Bad* means I do not prefer or desire it; I don't like it; I don't want it; I am unhappy with it.

9. Game-of-Life Law of Diversity

What I evaluate as *good* or *bad* may not be considered the same by others. That does not make either of us good or bad, right or wrong, or the things we evaluate intrinsically good or bad. We are simply expressing our preferences.

Differences in size, shape, speech, customs, race, disposition, behavior, religion, politics, and food choices are all forms of variety essential to the Game of Life for fun, freedom, exploration, adventure, and expansion.

Life would be dull with nothing to attract or repulse. The absence of likes or dislikes would present no opportunity for freedom of choice and the resultant fun opportunities.

9. Game-of-Life Law of Diversity

I observe the diversity I encounter and affirm:

- *It's all good!*
- *It's all for my benefit, whether I like it or not, whether I want it or not!*
- *It's OK because it's the way the Game of Life works.*
- *Variety contributes to my fun.*

10. GAME-OF-LIFE LAW OF EXPANSION

NASA-STScI

The imperative for expansion is built into every particle of the universe. Evolution constantly creates new life species. New galaxies continuously form and accelerate away from each other at increasing speed.

LAW of EXPANSION:
THE-FLOW of energy expands with infinite resources to meet the desires of every Game player.

---

10. Game-of-Life Law of Expansion

Notice there is dramatically more *stuff* on earth than a century ago. Where did the expansion of this stuff come from? *THE-FLOW* delivered things as manifestations in answer to the desires, envisions, and expectations of Earthlings as they played Life's Game by focusing on what they wanted.

When we desire, imagine, expect, and stay in *THE-FLOW,* the supply-chain physics and metaphysics built into the structure of Life's Game manifest our desires.

The Law of Expansion provides what is needed from its unlimited resources. Manifestations often seem miraculous because they are so perfectly meshed with the activities of other Game players as to arrive at just the right time and place to exceed our desires.

There is cooperation in the Game but no competition because resources expand to supply all desires.

Everyone has an equal chance to win by getting as much satisfaction,

10. Game-of-Life Law of Expansion

happiness, and material things as they choose by their thoughts.

Nothing is reduced or diluted as more people join the Game and tap into *THE-FLOW* energy field.

I envision *THE-FLOW* as a fountain fed by infinite Divine resources flowing from the Law of Expansion without limit to me and to all who accept it.

⚽ ⚽ ⚽

11. Game-of-Life Creator

A very, very long time ago, so long ago that it was before matter and time even existed, there was a bundle of consciousness. That's all there was, nothing else but the bundle, like an invisible cloud of massive, all-pervasive, conscious, multi-faceted thought-energy. Since this was all that existed, I'll call it *ALL*.

Since *ALL* is definitely a conscious personality, not a lifeless "it," I need a personal pronoun. *ALL* is neither male nor female, or non-binary in today's terms. In the absence of a singular, genderless personal pronoun in English, I will use the plural form *THEY, THEM, THEIR*.

11. Game-of-Life Creator

ALL thought: ***What fun it would be to make stuff.*** After much thought, *ALL* decided to make stuff composed of parts of *THEIR* consciousness energy that could vibrate and bind together to make other stuff.

ALL decided to create an immense complex *playground* for the consciousness energy *THEY* would spin out of *THEMSELVES*. Everything in the playground would connect by logic and be powered by mathematical laws of evolution and expansion.

ALL planned endless ways for *THEIR* energy to transform and reveal itself with different effects, bringing endless new things into existence. *ALL* planned all the processes, the interactions, what we would call the laws and rules, and decided to bundle them into the consciousness energy.

What fun to cause all this to come into existence and to watch it evolve and expand, *ALL* thought. Then ALL created the universe in a single flash.

11. Game-of-Life Creator

ALL is very pleased as *THEIR* playground evolves. When everything is prepared, as part of the plan, *ALL* fulfills *THEIR* mandate to expand by pulling off tiny droplets of *THEIR* consciousness energy identical in every way to *THEMSELVES*. In creating these *Droplets*, *ALL* retains every aspect of *THEIR* being. *ALL* continues undiminished.

The *ALL-Droplets* have all the powers and attributes of *ALL*, including the freedom to choose expansion by entry into the time-space physical playground of the universe to enjoy the experience for a limited time.

When the *Droplets* make the choice to play on planet Earth, *THEY* become *Players* in the Game of Life.

👀 👀 👀

12. GAME-OF-LIFE PLAYERS

As a developing embryo in our mother's womb, life-force energy enlivened us, a phenomenon that doctors, theologians, scientists, and philosophers attempt to explain with limited success.

I believe the correct explanation is an all-loving Divine Consciousness came to explore life on this planet by inserting a part of *THEMSELVES* into the clothing of a body to become the blended human that each one of us is, part Spirit and part material.

When *THEY* choose to enter the physical playground called Earth, *Droplets* of *ALL* continue being eternal, immaterial, and part of *ALL*. They add a physical aspect temporarily

12. Game-of-Life Players

for the adventure. These *Droplets* now have two energy vibrations: their physical mind-body and their *Droplet-ALL-consciousness.*

To make for a more interesting adventure, their new physical-mind component forgets all that their *Droplet-ALL-consciousness* knows. Thus, they can learn, develop desires, and experience adventures without the hindrance of prior memories.

We Earthlings are these composite physical-immaterial beings here for a lifetime as *PLAYERS* in the Game of Life.

We have all the powers of *ALL* to convert thought energy into physical form with the process *ALL* created and built into the physical universe.

12. Game-of-Life Players

That process, the *Law of Attraction*, causes energy vibrations of similar frequencies to attract, reinforce, and mutually amplify until they become strong enough to manifest into physical reality. How this works out for each of us is how we play the Game of Life.

Our *Droplet*-of-*ALL* part is always loving, never judging, and always guiding us toward the experiences and happiness we desire.

Inner-Spirit is the name I use for this Divine part that powers our body with life-force, our mind with intuition and inspiration, and our emotions with feedback guidance.

Our *Inner-Spirit*'s power is unlimited. We can heal our body of any discomfort and invoke whatever miracles we choose to believe and expect. We can be, do, or have anything we desire and accept.

Many humans have realized life on earth for a few years is a game. While some thought it a competitive game, the wise ones realized it is non-

12. Game-of-Life Players

competitive and a highly mental game, much like putting a puzzle together.

Why do we put puzzles together? Because it is enjoyable.

Why is putting puzzles together so enjoyable?

Because *ALL* is ever learning and expanding, growing in knowledge and skill, and finding pleasure in that expansion. *ALL* finds satisfaction in accomplishment and moving up to ever-greater challenges.

Because we are part of *ALL*, *mini-ALLs*, our consciousness gets pleasure and satisfaction from games. That's why so many people love sports. Games and fun are part of the *ALL-Consciousness* that we participate in as the Game of Life continues.

12. Game-of-Life Players

Body

Because computer designers made computers like us, technology can be a good analogy to understand ourselves.

Computers come in many styles, features, and manufacturers. Your computer has a protective case with a logo indicating its origin. We each enter this world with a distinctive DNA structure inherited from our parents, with hundreds of epigenetic switches to turn the DNA on or off with factors under our control. We bear the logo of our parents in every cell.

Our five senses are like the screen, keyboard, microphone, and speaker to get information into and out of our brain CPU (central processing unit). Our brain, like a computer, emits electromagnetic energy waves from the firings of electrical charges between nerve cells triggered by focus, stimuli, or memory. These energy vibrations go out and match up with other waves of the same frequency.

Mind

Our consciousness is a complex, little-understood faculty enabling us to think, to remember, to imagine, to be aware of the world, our experiences, and of ourselves. Mind is throughout the body with each cell contributing, the primary location in the brain and a secondary concentration in the heart.

Our mind is categorized into three aspects of **conscious, subconscious,** and **superconscious**, each with different effects in Game-of-Life play.

Conscious Mind

Philosophers have speculated for centuries about consciousness and mind. Shakespeare's plays, poetry, books on religion and spirituality contain allusions to consciousness without any clear explanation.

The brain is the physical device for consciousness but not consciousness itself, somewhat like the computer

12. Game-of-Life Players

memory chip is the physical device that holds the song but is not the song. Consciousness remains a mystery, but you decided to read this book with your conscious mind.

It is the kitchen where thoughts are cooked up. It is the mixer of inputs from our senses, habits, beliefs, external thought energy, inspirations, and imagination. It is our decision control center where we exercise our freedom to think and to act and to enforce "willpower."

Because staying alive is its highest priority, it resists change from a fear that the unknown may be worse than the present experience. It goes offline during sleep and partly offline with closed-eye deep breathing and autosuggestion.

We play the Game of Life mostly in our conscious mind because this is where our decisions about thoughts originate. This is the center for our thoughts that are the driving force of our play in Life's Game.

12. Game-of-Life Players

Our conscious mind is like an app (application program) focused on one task at a time. The Law of Attraction will bring more of the thoughts that are occupying our conscious mind. Our life follows the natural flow of thoughts evoking emotions that lead to actions to cause results.

Deciding to keep or change thoughts is the primary Gameplay function of the conscious mind. The choices can keep us *BALANCED*, cause a whirlpool of *DOWN* emotions, or invite a joyous spiral of *UP* emotions.

Subconscious Mind

The subconscious mind is the human operating system, a powerful assistant to our conscious mind. Just as a computer operating system handles the behind-the-scenes tasks, our subconscious handles hundreds of necessary tasks based on its settings in our control center. Most tasks controlled by the subconscious are hidden from our conscious mind.

12. Game-of-Life Players

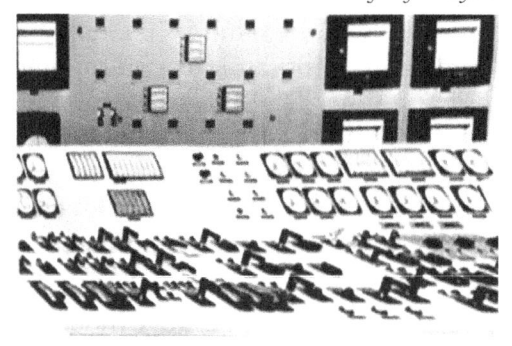

Our subconscious runs all our body functions and muscle-contraction neuron programs called habits for our dozens of learned response patterns. Its expandable memory stores every sensation, word heard or spoken, every image seen or imagined. It never goes offline. It creates our dreams while our conscious mind sleeps.

We play much of our Game of Life from automatic programs in our subconscious control center, enabling our conscious mind to focus on its important task of controlling thoughts and decisions. We have hundreds of involuntary responses, like subroutines, small programs of

12. Game-of-Life Players

stored nerve and muscle responses that get us through most of life's activities, sometimes resulting in spontaneous emotions.

Our subconscious mind holds our database of beliefs. They are both the starting material and filter for our thoughts. We accepted most of our beliefs during childhood. Many may remain hidden from our view. We can choose to expose, evaluate, and change them. Coaching can assist in reprogramming buried memories.

Understanding our subconscious is important to playing the Game well because our beliefs, habits, and reactions arise involuntarily from the subconscious. After they show themselves in our consciousness, we get to choose between keeping and feeding them, or not.

Whatever thoughts and emotions we keep, the Law of Attraction will feed with more of the same and they will grow.

12. Game-of-Life Players

Superconscious Mind

Our superconscious is the eternal divine *Droplet* that took on flesh to become human, who will return to pure spirit when our body dies, who connects us to Divine Intelligence and all non-physical, past, present, and future. It is another name for our *Inner-Spirit*, that part always loving us, never judging, and always finding the easiest way to lead us to what we desire and to be happy.

When we notice we like something, our superconscious *Inner-Spirit* accepts our desire and taps into *THE-FLOW* to prepare connections, resources, and everything needed to deliver our desire. Our superconscious leads us to the manifestation of our desires with urgings, inspirations, ideas, something we read, a photo, or anything to move us in the direction of allowing, of

12. Game-of-Life Players

opening ourselves to *THE-FLOW*. When we are ready, our superconscious funnels *THE-FLOW* to us to manifest our Law of Attraction results.

As we play the Game of Life, our superconscious acts as our GPS, always prompting us with thoughts for what to do next. Following these promptings will be the easiest way to get what we want.

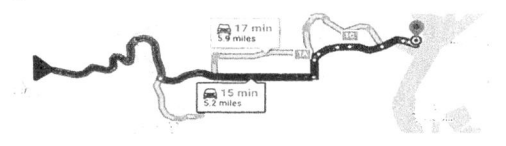

It is OK if we ignore a prompt. Just like a GPS, our superconscious will adjust the route to our desire and give us new promptings for the adjusted path. Also like a GPS, it never gets angry or impatient, never tires of calculating a rerouted path, and never ceases giving us promptings toward our desired goal.

Our superconscious connects us to everyone who ever lived or still lives. Our superconscious is our direct

12. Game-of-Life Players

channel for communication with deceased relatives, past experts in whatever skill we desire, or anyone we wish to contact.

Our superconscious connects us to the spirit part of our living relatives and friends. Our superconscious is like our internet connection, providing a communication channel to resources beyond imagination.

Most people have experienced knowing the exact time something happened to someone to whom they were energetically connected. I've received numerous calls just as I was thinking about calling that person, a sure sign of the communication between my superconscious and theirs.

Our superconscious is our power source for miracles. Since this is our active portal to divinity, it is infinite and all-powerful. It can heal our body from any disease. It taps into *THE-FLOW* to perform whatever miracles we are willing to allow and accept. Our superconscious mind continues as unchanged pure positive spirit energy when it will leave our body at Game Transformation.

Habits

Habits are programmed automatic responses stored in our subconscious as nervous system programs. We love habits because they free our conscious mind from repetitive tasks essential for daily living. Once the pattern of repetition is mastered, our conscious mind sends the control of a repetitive activity down to our subconscious as a habit program we can run whenever we need without requiring conscious thought.

Walking is a habit. As an infant, I spent conscious energy for many weeks learning how to walk. I concentrated on firing neurons to move muscles in a pattern that imitated what I saw adults doing. Encouragement from Mom and Dad motivated me to keep trying to get the pattern right even though I kept falling.

12. Game-of-Life Players

Finally, I figured it out and wobbled my first steps. With more practice, my walking got smoother, but still needed my conscious effort. Eventually, walking needed less conscious thought as it became a routine program habit.

Now everything about walking no longer needs conscious thought. Once I decide with my conscious mind where I want to walk, my subconscious autopilot uses my stored walking program to manage all the details of the proper sequence of muscle firings. There are even subroutines for balance recovery when I lean too much left, right, forward, or backward. Subconscious habits handle much of my life activity.

Emotions

Our emotions are the complex interplay between our body, mind, and *Inner-Spirit*.

Sometimes the thought comes first, like sadness when we watch movie scenes of suffering. Sometimes an emotion can seem like it *came-out-of-the-blu*e when it comes from a subconscious reaction auto-program.

Awareness of our emotions and what they convey is essential to successful Gameplay. They provide information about how aligned our thinking is with the thinking of our *Inner-Spirit* so we can decide whether to change our thoughts or keep them.

12. Game-of-Life Players

Like a car's gas gauge, emotions are neither good nor bad, but provide valuable information for what to do next.

← KEEP THOUGHT | **?** | **CHANGE THOUGHT →**

Wherever I focus my thoughts, my *Inner-Spirit* focuses also, but always in the most loving, beneficial way. If I have thoughts of judgment, fear, frustration, anger, or any type of low vibration frequency thoughts, my *Inner-Spirit* does not have similar thoughts, and I can tell by how I feel. I "feel bad," an unpleasant low-frequency emotion.

Our *Inner-Spirit* constantly loves us, guides us to allow *THE-FLOW* to achieve what we desire, and never judges us. When our thoughts align with what our *Inner-Spirit* is thinking, we "feel good" (pleasing emotions in the higher frequencies).

⚽ ⚽ ⚽

13. Life Emotion Frequency Scale

+ 7. Joy, Love, Freedom, Knowledge, Appreciation, Empowerment
+ 6. Passion
+ 5. Enthusiasm, Eagerness, Happiness
+ 4. Positive Expectation, Belief
+ 3. Optimism
+ 2. Hopefulness
+ 1. Contentment, Satisfaction, Replenishment

> 0. –Release–Trust–Let-Go transition

– 1. Boredom, Stagnation, Stuck
– 2. Pessimism
– 3. Frustration, Irritation, Impatience
– 4. Overwhelmed
– 5. Disappointed, Dissatisfied
– 6. Doubt
– 7. Worry, Anxiety
– 8. Blame
– 9. Discouragement
– 10. Anger
– 11. Revenge, Judgment, Righteousness
– 12. Hatred, Rage
– 13. Jealousy
– 14. Insecurity, Guilt, Unworthiness
– 15. Fear, Depression, Powerlessness, Grief, Despair, Helplessness

(Adapted from ABRAHAM-HICKS: signs, positions, & numbers show relative frequency.)

13. Life Emotion Frequency Scale

EMOTION SCALE = HOTEL PROFILE

I imagine the emotional scale as the profile of an international hotel with level zero as the *ground* floor at street level. The better-feeling emotions are on the upper, positive-numbered levels. They have windows that let in the sunshine that signals I am on the route to things I desire. The level seven penthouse is where I want to stay as often as possible. When I find myself on a negative-number basement parking level, my unpleasant emotion means I have a low-frequency vibration, am off my path, and attracting unwanted things. The deeper the level, the farther off my path and the farther I must climb

13. Life Emotion Frequency Scale

to get up to the daylight, the joy, and the things I desire.

Emotions are indicators to tell me where I am so I can decide what to do next. If I enjoy an emotion, I can keep the thought that generated the emotion and attract more like it. If I'm not enjoying the emotion, I can change my thought to one that will create a more pleasing emotion.

⬅ KEEP THOUGHT ? CHANGE THOUGHT ➡

I get back on my path by replacing the thought with a different thought that stimulates a better-feeling emotion. This process is an important Game skill everyone can learn.

No emotion is negative in the sense of BAD. All emotions are beneficial (GOOD) because they show my vibration match/mismatch with the vibration of my all-loving *Inner-Spirit*. They give me the information to adjust my thoughts to play my best Game.

13. Life Emotion Frequency Scale

My journey to understand the role of emotions in Life's Game did not come easy. My training had taught me to stuff my emotions, especially anger. After Dona passed, I entered a period of grief healing and found *Grief Yoga*, a yoga routine with added body moves to release emotions.

Besides releasing grief, it made me aware of the anger I had never acknowledged. Though not writing prose or poetry at the time, I was inspired to write this poem following one of the yoga workouts:

Anger? None I Thought!

Duncan Tooley, 2015

13. Life Emotion Frequency Scale

Anger? None, I thought!
I have no anger about my loss.
Not at her; not at doctors, not at God.
Not at life; not at death; not at me.
No. Not at anyone; not at all!

Grief Yoga they call it.
Boxing, gardening, trash removal,
    sanitation
Tuned to heartbeat, breath, vocal
    vibration.

Anger? None, I thought!
Then I found
a tiny insult here,
a small disappointment there,
a minor refusal,
a petite withdrawal,
a lack expressed,
a lie,
a layoff,
a credit denial,
a love request rejected.

A stream of little angers
Discounted, swallowed, buried taut,
Broke the dam,
The flood belied
Anger? None I thought.

13. Life Emotion Frequency Scale

Yank, pull, toss.
Weed, groan, eject.
Laugh, nonsense-speak.
Vibrate, twirl, breathe.

Cry, clear, heal, forgive.
Grow, realize, restore.
Move, twist, expand, breathe.
Tears release yet more.

De-anger, de-grieve.
Forgive myself, breathe.
Do it on a yoga mat.

Anger? None, I thought!
Now.......
Anger?
Less, I know!

Growth began. I started to identify and accept my emotions as beneficial information.

⚽

I keep the *LIFE Emotion Frequency Scale* handy for reference when I check how I am feeling. I tell my coaching clients to keep a copy of the scale where they will see it daily as their

13. Life Emotion Frequency Scale

reminder that emotions are gauges that tell:

- How aligned their thoughts are with their *Inner-Spirit's* thoughts.
- The quality of their Gameplay at that moment.
- What will be manifesting in their future: things they will like or things they won't like.

GET YOUR COPY of **the Game-of-Life Emotion Frequency Scale:**

Tear out the extra copy from the back of this book to keep as a reminder, or download and print a larger copy:

www.dtooley.com/lifesplaybook/emo-scale.pdf

14. Game-of-Life Rule #1

Games have rules and referees to enforce them. While no player has any choice about laws, players are free to play by the rules or violate them, to observe them, or *break* them. The referee's role is to enforce the rules and the consequences for violating them.

In addition to the four laws, the Game of Life has three rules.

> Rule #1:
> ## Accept and love myself.

I am my *Inner-Spirit*, a droplet of the Divine, clothed in temporal flesh. The Divine is all love, all good, and so

14. Game-of-Life Rule #1

is every Game-Player as a participant in the Divine. As such, we all deserve everything this space-time world has to offer. We are worthy and deserving of health, wealth, freedom, fun, companionship, happiness, love, joy, miracles, and all good things.

Every player in Life's Game gets the freedom to choose to love themself and accept the divine creature they are. If they put themself down or think they are not good enough, they tell themself an enormous lie. Each of us is divine, worthy, and deserving of everything life offers.

We all came to play Life's Game. Bumps in the road, stumbles, errors, and mistaken turns are learning experiences of normal Gameplay. They do not negate our goodness and worthiness. My *Inner-Spirit* loves the human part of me, no matter what I do. That's true for every player's *Inner-Spirit*.

14. Game-of-Life Rule #1

Our BIRTHRIGHT:

We are worthy and deserving of all goods things THE-FLOW can deliver, anything we want

to BE,

DO,

or HAVE.

15. Game-of-Life Rule #2

The second rule depends on the first because it asks that we treat others with the same dignity, care, and attention we have for ourselves.

If I do not love and respect myself, it is impossible for me to spread any love and respect to anyone else.

15. Game-of-Life Rule #2

> Rule #2 The Golden Rule:
> Treat others as I want them to treat me.

The Law of Diversity means everyone has the freedom and right to play their Game as they choose. Everyone deserves my respect even if their path is dramatically different from my choices. The Game is to be played as a team. The energy doesn't flow properly if I try to do every play by myself.

16. GAME-OF-LIFE RULE #3

> Rule #3:
> Have FUN!

The Game of Life is all about FUN.

Every player decided to come to Earth's playground for FUN.

Have as much FUN as possible.

17. GAME-OF-LIFE GAMEPLAY

In Life's Game, we play directly with *THE-FLOW* energy field through our thoughts, imagination, expectations, and movement.

Although we are in a bath of energy vibrations, only those that exactly match the frequency of our thoughts at that moment affect our Gameplay.

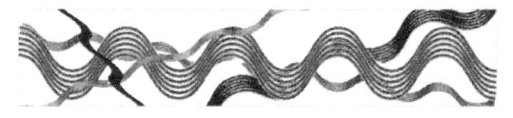

The Law of Attraction matches us with people, circumstances, and events of the same vibration frequency as ours, delivering them at just the right time. The limitless resources of *THE-FLOW* provide what we request by the vibration energy we radiate.

17. Game-of-Life GamePlay

Playing a physical game like football involves not only *my* actions, but also those of the *other players* on both teams, the field conditions, the spectators, and the weather.

Playing the Game of Life similarly involves other people, circumstances, and events, each radiating their unique energy into *THE-FLOW*.

The Law of Attraction then delivers to each player only those Game experiences and manifestations that match their energy frequency.

We play Life's Game primarily in our conscious mind because it's where we exercise the freedom to imagine, keep a thought, or change a thought, the essential activity in Life's Gameplay. Life is not primarily physical action; it is decisions about thoughts. Each thought

17. Game-of-Life GamePlay

choice summons more similar thoughts of the same energy frequency.

Our thought vibrations affect all the cells in our body. Depending on their frequency, they can cause illness and pain, or they can turn pain off and heal illness.

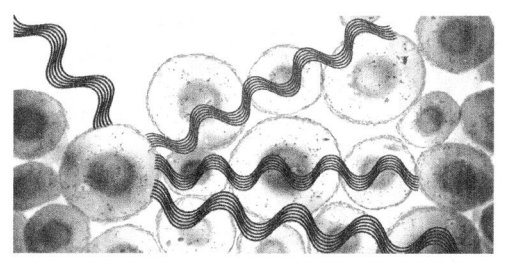

We are already our own physician-healer or poisoner by our focus on either wellness or illness with its effect on our cells.

There are cosmic consequences to what we broadcast in our personal energy signature of thoughts, feelings, and expectations because the Law of Attraction unwaveringly delivers with a guarantee: What we think about, comes about!

17. Game-of-Life GamePlay

Gameplay is like using a Global Positioning System (GPS). My phone GPS app calculates my location from multiple satellite signals and shows it on a map. When I enter a destination address, my GPS program calculates multiple paths from a roadmap database and suggests an optimized route (blue line) with turn instructions.

Similarly, my desires emit thought energy vibrations in Life's Game. My *Inner-Spirit* accepts my desires as GPS-like destinations, then calculates the routes to all destinations, and suggests the next moves along an optimized path to each desire.

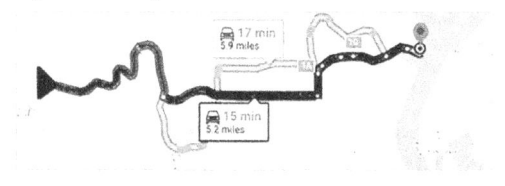

These suggestions come in the form of impulses, thoughts, intuition, dreams, and physical cues like a song lyric or phrase in a book, a photo, a pet's actions, or a word someone says.

17. Game-of-Life GamePlay

Just as my vehicle's progress on my GPS map is updated, my emotions provide Gameplay feedback. High-frequency, good-feeling emotions signal I am on my optimal route, *on the blue line*. Unpleasant, low-frequency emotions signal I am off the path.

If I get off my path, my *Inner-Spirit* GPS-wizard calculates a revised route to get me back headed toward my destination desires and gives me updated suggestions as intuitive urgings as immediately and blamelessly as my phone GPS.

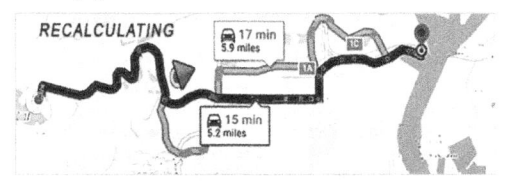

When my life experiences change or add to my destination desires, my *Inner-Spirit*-GPS-wizard revises my destination list and computes a new route optimized for my current position and readiness for each destination desire to become manifested.

17. Game-of-Life GamePlay

My primary Gameplay is deciding to *keep* or *change* a thought.

By doing so, I take control of the fun, adventure, satisfaction, and outcomes in Life's Game by managing my thoughts and emotions.

I know that whatever will show up will be because I created it with my thoughts.

⚽

Eva and I learned the frequency-matched basis of manifestations from our teachers and mentors. We don't understand the mechanics, but because we continually experience it in our lives, we are certain it is true. We accept it as the way reality is. Striving to improve our game-playing skills has led to magical results. Here is the story of a recent validation of the Laws of the Game at work in our lives:

Just weeks before a workshop Eva would teach in Provence, France, she

17. Game-of-Life GamePlay

broke her leg, requiring a steel bolt up into her hip socket. We envisioned her traveling and teaching despite the predicted extended recovery time with a walker. We would need help to board the trains because I also have balance issues and wear dual drop-foot braces.

We remained confident we would obtain Paris train station *Accès Plus* wheelchair assistance despite our futile search for the prerequisite French cell phone for an advance request.

Arriving two hours early at the entrance to Paris *Gare de Lyon* trusting assistance would find us, I pulled a roller suitcase in each hand with computers in my backpack as Eva walked slowly with a cane. When we found the elevators inoperable, the driver I flagged down hopped out of his car, motioned for us to follow him onto the escalator, grabbed both our bags, deposited them at the top of the escalator, smiled, and refused payment.

Inside, I asked a man with a red vest where we could get assistance boarding.

17. Game-of-Life GamePlay

He pointed and began giving us directions, hesitated, changed his mind (was it his intuition?), and said, "Follow me."

Walking slowly for a dozen minutes behind the man with *Chef Incident Gare* on his vest, we arrived at the *Accès Plus* office, the destination for our unsent request.

After a long conversation, the person inside leaped up and put Eva in a wheelchair. The two men took us to an empty train, helped us board, stowed our luggage, and seated us.

We were the first to board an empty train scheduled to depart forty

17. Game-of-Life GamePlay

minutes later. When the train arrived in Avignon, two *Accès Plus* men with wheelchairs escorted us from the train.

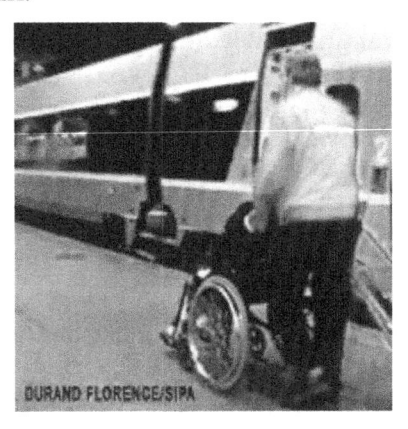

We couldn't have been happier. We knew the *Law of Attraction* delivered the assistance we wanted because we envisioned what we needed, had positive expectations, and stayed focused on the desired outcome, in high-frequency emotions.

The results matched the radiated energy of our focused expectations:

17. Game-of-Life GamePlay

the right people in the right places at the right times to help us on and off the trains.

Our mentors said it would always be like this. We have accumulated sufficient experiences to be certain our desires will always manifest when we listen to our *Inner-Spirit* intuition, pause to prepare, and stay focused with expectant trust and in higher frequency emotions.

The results are the same for every player who has tuned into working with the laws and rules of the Game of Life. I keep meeting others who recount similar amazing, often miraculous, experiences.

👁 👁 👁

18. Game-of-Life Scoring

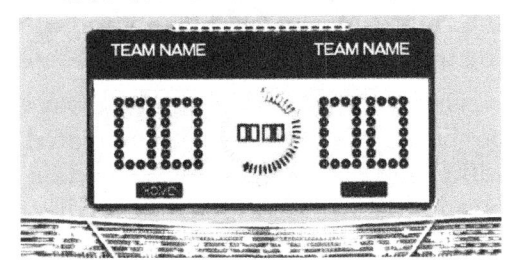

Score is kept in games to inform the players and spectators who is winning during play and who is the winner at the end of the game.

Because every player in the Game of Life can win all the satisfaction, fun, and joy they choose without affecting other players, no external public score is needed. There is no competition in Life's Game because each player has sole control of their gameplay, and the Law of Expansion increases the resources to supply every player.

Each player supports their team members by the observance of the Golden Rule. They give the love, freedom, and support they desire for

18. Game-of-Life Scoring

themselves to every other player, allowing each player to resolve their own happiness score.

Each player can determine their instantaneous score of how well they are doing at that moment in their Game of Life by observing their current emotion's position on the emotion frequency scale.

Positive-level emotions mean game-playing well at that moment. Negative-level emotions mean not playing well and creating things undesired for the future.

⚽ ⚽ ⚽

19. Game-of-Life Referee

The Law of Attraction becomes the automatic referee when a Game player breaks a Game rule. It delivers to the player, as it always does, things, people, and events that match the player's frequency. It loops back to the player whatever is sent out, just like a boomerang comes back to its thrower.

Those who radiate the energy of love and joy get the energy of love and joy coming back to them *(Heaven-on-Earth)*. Those who radiate the energy of hate get the energy of hate coming

19. Game-of-Life Referee

back to them *(Hell-on-Earth)*. Those who do not love themselves and treat their neighbor without love will get the absence of love boomeranging back to them.

Reward and penalty in this life are automatic and guaranteed because they are built into Life's Game. This popular wisdom nugget confirms the Game result: ***What goes around, comes around!***

We can recover from our mistakes and rule infractions. Once we replace self-loathing thoughts with self-acceptance (Rule#1), treat others more lovingly (Rule#2), and stop doing things we don't like (Rule#3), better-feeling emotions will indicate progress back on the *blue line* path to our desired destinations.

19. Game-of-Life Referee

When experienced players stumble, slip, break a rule, or make an error, they say to themselves, "It's OK; It means I'm still human! This is all part of the Game. I forgive myself!"

FORGIVE YOURSELF

They get up, start anew, climb back up the emotion scale, release low-frequency beliefs, cross the zero-level threshold on the emotion scale by forgiving themselves and others, and continue Life's journey to develop their Game skills.

☙ ☙ ☙

20. Game-of-Life Skills

The best players in any game are the ones who hone their Gameplay skills. Because the Game of Life is played in the energy environment of *THE-FLOW*, life's successful players hone their skills that optimize their high-frequency energy flow.

20. Game-of-Life Skills

In football, the winning play is kicking the ball into the goal for a score. Soccer players strive to improve their kicking skills.

In baseball, the winning play is hitting a home run. Baseball players strive to improve their batting skills.

In the Game of Life, the winning play is *noticing* emotion triggered by a thought and then *deciding* to keep or change the thought.

20. Game-of-Life Skills

Game of Life players strive to improve their emotion awareness and mental focus skills.

I learned to nurture four Gameplay mental skills:

- o Listen to Intuition;
- o Pause & prepare;
- o Stay focused;
- o Learn from emotion.

▸*LISTEN TO MY INTUITION:* Intuition is my inner quiet voice that answers when I ask for guidance. It is a sense of knowing without conscious

20. Game-of-Life Skills

reasoning, the gut feeling, sudden insight, urging, or my inner wisdom, sometimes revealed through tingling, goosebumps, tears, or a knot in my stomach. It is guidance from my Inner-Spirit-GPS-Coach.

I practice listening.

▸*PAUSE & PREPARE*: I find my Gameplay is better, and my enjoyment is greater when I pause and prepare before making a decision or taking an action. I pause to ask myself:

o   Why this decision or action now?

o   What outcome do I want?

o   What does my Intuition tell me?

o   Does it feel good (high vibration)?

20. Game-of-Life Skills

My answers help me decide the best choice for everyone involved.

▸ *STAY FOCUSED:* The Law of Attraction brings a match to my thoughts but rarely instantly. It takes about 17 seconds of *focused* continued thought on a subject before the Law brings more similar thoughts. I am pleased about this delay because it gives me a time buffer decide if I like a thought that pops into my mind. If I don't like the way it feels, I can discard it before it attracts more like it.

When I stay focused on a subject for over a minute, things to deliver the manifestation are gathered and added to my destinations.

20. Game-of-Life Skills

Once I choose a decision, I next make it my *best* by putting all my energy into it, believing in it, going *"all in,"* and expecting its results.

I know any out-of-focus thoughts or arguments against my decision guarantee I won't get what I want and won't be happy. I also know it's OK to change my mind to another decision after I give my initial decision a fair opportunity to deliver results.

Expert players in the Game of Life know the Law of Attraction works whether they are focused or not.

The-FLOW

When they focus their intention and attention, they experience being in *THE-FLOW,* often creating surprise, sometimes miraculous, manifestations.

20. Game-of-Life Skills

▸ *LEARN FROM MY EMOTIONS:* Emotions give instantaneous feedback on how well I am playing Life's Game. To learn from that information, I developed this habit:

a) Keep the Emotional Frequency Scale nearby as a handy reference to check how I'm feeling.

b) Notice my emotion and name it.

c) Check its frequency level on the emotion scale.

d) Construct a thought that elicits an emotion on the next higher level.

e) Say, imagine, or intensely think that new thought until it generates a higher frequency feeling.

f) Repeat, moving up the scale one level each time until satisfied.

I recommend the above skill-building practice. Download your copy of the Life Emotion Frequency Scale here:

www.dtooley.com/lifesplaybook/emo-scale.pdf

21. Game-of-Life Coach

Coach says:

Focus
Focus
Focus

Game coaches help their players build game skills. Great coaches assist players to reach their full potential by teaching specific skills and giving feedback, encouragement, and guidance.

Human coaches are an important component of life-skills building because they are physically visible, can demonstrate the skills, and can hold players accountable.

Each player in Life's Game receives subtle GPS-like guidance instructions to all their desired destinations from their *Inner-Spirit* Game Coach, who provides play-by-play feedback through inspiration, emotions, and intuition

21. Game-of-Life Coach

rather than through movement of a vehicle icon on a GPS map.

Wherever a Life-player focuses thought, their *Inner-Spirit* coach focuses also, but always in the most loving way that organizes the resources in Life's Game to meet their Life-player's desires.

My *Inner-Spirit* coach, whom I call *Soaring Eagle,* encourages me along the easiest path to manifestation of my desires by giving me hints: a word, dream, picture, phrase, billboard, event, an idea *out of the blue*. Often, *Soaring Eagle* seems to supply the words or thoughts for my writing as a *download.*

On a morning walk, exercising with dumbbell hand weights, my arms became excessively fatigued. I hid the dumbbells behind a tree and continued to the end of my usual walking loop.

21. Game-of-Life Coach

Absorbed in the pleasantness of the day and the ocean view on my way back, I walked past the tree without a thought about the weights.

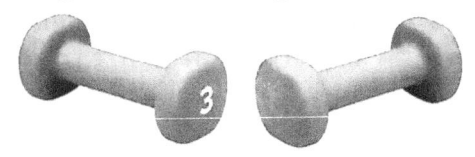

A few minutes later, a man walked toward me pumping his arms up and down with small dumbbells, reminding me to retrieve my weights.

This was another example of the Law of Attraction working in my life to match up my desire with this man's arm-strengthening desire, (the same frequency). My inner coach, Soaring Eagle, arranged the timing to remind me to retrieve my weights.

It was no coincidence because I never saw anyone walking with weights before or after that day. My inner coach worked with the Game-of-Life Laws to deliver what I wanted.

☻ ☻ ☻

22. GAME-OF-LIFE TRANSFORMATION

At some point, the Game will change. Regardless of how each of us plays the Game, we will certainly end this lifetime, shed our body, and leave behind everything associated with it, like pain, age, illness, and possessions.

This is not the end of Life's Game. Instead, the Game is transformed in appearance and gameplay when our physical body and eternal Divine *Consciousness-Droplet* separate at what is called *death*. The Divine consciousness that empowered the body continues to play the Game without the physical

22. Game-of-Life Transformation

limitations as the body returns to its original basic chemical elements.

We came to enjoy playing the Game and *play* is what we will have done with our every breath and thought, creating our earthly heaven or hell. We will have played the Game with every choice we made. By doing so, we will have contributed to the Universe's expansion by desiring, envisioning, expecting, creating, and bringing forth what did not exist previously.

We won't be judged, punished, or rewarded for anything we did. As we played the Game, the Laws built into the Game ensured that we received our appropriate reward during our Earth lifetime.

If we broke the Game Rules, we didn't get as much enjoyment; it wasn't as much fun. We probably experienced more pain and suffering. Our choices caused it.

If we observed the Rules, we experienced happiness and the love

22. Game-of-Life Transformation

of others. We contributed to the expansion of the universe and the elevation of the aggregate vibration frequency of mankind. We fulfilled our purpose in incarnating.

We certainly will NOT be sent to a non-existent Hell or Purgatory. We will continue as pure positive spirit energy for eternity as our *Inner-Spirit* non-physical Droplet of the Divine.

We will connect gloriously with all our angels, family, friends, and mentors while continuing to play an active role in participating with those still alive on Earth.

We may choose to return to play another Game.

☙ ☙ ☙

23. GAME-OF-LIFE LEGACY

After a game, the legacies remain, the final score, the photographs, the trophies, perhaps a successful new play, and the memories of special moments. Together these contribute to education and encouragement for current and future players.

It's the same for Life's Game. We inherited a rich legacy from our ancestors and direct family. We will want to pass to our descendants the life lessons we learned and the plays and tips we found useful for our Gameplay.

23. Game-of-Life Legacy

For our future progeny, we will each have the unique legacy we are forming right now as we play Life's Game.

I invite you to reflect on how you will transmit your legacy of play in Life's Game.

- Will you prepare a list of what worked and what didn't?
- Will you pass this playbook along to them?
- Will you write your own story of how you played and what you learned?

24. GAME-OF-LIFE HACK

HACK (verb):

- Find a short-cut, mechanism, or path.

- Synonyms: Navigate, Maneuver, Manipulate, Manage, Negotiate, Play, Surmount, Master.

HACK steps to manifest *whatever you want,* miracles included:

1. Decide what you want. Notice how you feel when you think about it. If you feel good, it matches your *Inner-Spirit's* view that this desire benefits you. Be as specific yet good-feeling as possible. (If it feels unpleasant, it does not match the frequency of your *Inner-Spirit*. Change any ill-feeling thought).

24. Game-of-Life HACK

2. Envision/Embellish. Imagine the details, all aspects of what you want, and select those aspects that make you feel best. Add them to your detailed specification of what you want.

3. Ask for it. Again, make it as specific as you can imagine. Ask with expectancy that it will be given to you. Make the asking more powerful by feeling the emotion of enjoying what you ask.

4. Expect. Believe without any trace of doubt that it is coming, that it will happen. Instead of saying "I believe," say "I know; I'm convinced; I'm certain." Talk about it. Tell others that it is on its way. Think, dream, write, speak, and sing about it.

You are guaranteed the efficacy of the hack process:

> *"Truly I say to you, whoever says to this mountain, 'Be taken up and cast into the sea,' and does not doubt in his heart, but believes that what he says is going to happen, it will be granted him."* --Mark 11:23

5. Be grateful. Say often: *I am grateful the Universe is sending what I ask or something even better!*

6. Allow it to come to you. Know that you are worthy, no matter how outrageous or impossible it seems and whatever others have told you. Miracles are your birthright.

7. Respond to the promptings. Signs, thoughts, dreams, and ideas will urge you to do something related to your desire. Respond to the people, opportunities, and events that support your desire. This is how you allow it to come to you.

👁 👁 👁

When I thought my writing was complete, my *Inner-Spirit* told me to add a chapter for his personal message to you, dear reader. It follows as the postscript.

25. POSTSCRIPT

> "Pay attention to the inner thoughts and urgings you call *INTUITION*.
>
> "Intuition comes from your *Inner-Spirit*, forever loving you, wanting your happiness above all else, and prompting you like a GPS to the easiest path for all the things you desire from this lifetime.
>
> "Ask your *Inner-Spirit* for a name and daily coaching advice in playing Life's Game."
>
> — *Soaring Eagle*

About the Author

Duncan Tooley is a hypnotherapist, wellness & transformation coach, artist, and author of two books: *60-Second Pain Turn Down* and *End Pain & Feel Great Again*.

His quest to uncover the rules of life led him beyond his roots as a monk, artist, physics teacher, and computer engineer into the realm of body, mind, and spirit as a clinical hypnotherapist, healer, and life coach. This book fulfills his desire to provide players of all ages a paradigm to understand and master Life's Game.

He plays, coaches, envisions, and writes with visual artist and author Eva Margueriette in their studio overlooking the ocean near Los Angeles.

News/Workshops/Coaching:

www.lifesplaybook.duncantooley.com/info

email: life@duncantooley.com

Let's Play!

EXTRA GAME EMOTION FREQUENCY SCALE

The following page is a copy of the *Game-of-Life Emotion Frequency Scale* (with instructions on the reverse side) placed here for easy removal from the book.

Place it where you will see it daily as a reminder that your emotions are gauges that tell:

- How aligned your thoughts are with your Inner-Spirit's thoughts.
- Your quality of Gameplay at that moment.
- What's coming to manifest in your future: things you will like or things you won't like.

You always have the option to climb higher on the scale by thinking thoughts of higher frequency. (Hint: Use the instructions on the back of the Scale).

Life's Emotion Frequency Scale

+ 7. Joy, Love, Freedom, Knowledge, Appreciation, Empowerment
+ 6. Passion
+ 5. Enthusiasm, Eagerness, Happiness
+ 4. Positive Expectation, Belief
+ 3. Optimism
+ 2. Hopefulness
+ 1. Contentment, Satisfaction, Replenishment

> 0. –Release–Trust–Let-Go transition

- 1. Boredom, Stagnation, Stuck
- 2. Pessimism
- 3. Frustration, Irritation, Impatience
- 4. Overwhelmed
- 5. Disappointed, Dissatisfied
- 6. Doubt
- 7. Worry, Anxiety
- 8. Blame
- 9. Discouragement
- 10. Anger
- 11. Revenge, Judgment, Righteousness
- 12. Hatred, Rage
- 13. Jealousy
- 14. Insecurity, Guilt, Unworthiness
- 15. Fear, Depression, Powerlessness, Grief, Despair, Helplessness

---

(Adapted from ABRAHAM-HICKS: signs, positions, & numbers show relative frequency.)

Transform your Future:

CHANGE THOUGHT →

No matter how an emotion arises or how strong it might be, if you are not enjoying your emotion, you can change it by changing the thought triggering it.

Climb up the Emotion Scale one level at a time:

a) Notice your emotion and name it.

b) Note its level on the emotion scale.

c) Construct a thought that generates an emotion on the next higher level.

d) Say or intensely think that thought until you feel the higher emotion.

e) Repeat, moving up the scale one level at a time until you feel good.

Made in United States
Orlando, FL
09 June 2024